Zoospeak

Gordon Meade

with

Jo-Anne McArthur

E

Enthusiastic Press

ISBN: 978-1-9161130-4-6

For Wilma and Sophie,
and in memory of Lesley Herford.

Contents

Part Three: 2016 (i)

Brown Bear, Denmark, 2016
Red Fox, Lithuania, 2016
Orangutan, Denmark, 2016
Amur Leopard, France, 2016
Asian Elephant, Slovenia, 2016
Snow Leopard, Lithuania, 2016
Chimpanzee, Denmark, 2016
Leopards, Germany, 2016
Western Lowland Gorilla, Poland, 2016
Brown Bear, Croatia, 2016
Sand Tiger Shark, Canada, 2016
Burrowing Owl, Denmark, 2016

Part Four: 2016 (ii)

Lynx, Denmark, 2016
White Tiger, France, 2016
Lion, Croatia, 2016
Baltic Grey Seal, Lithuania, 2016
California Sea Lion, Denmark, 2016
Pileated Gibbon, France, 2016
Green Iguana, France, 2016
Plains Buffalo, France, 2016
Arctic Wolves, Lithuania, 2016
Toucan, Croatia, 2016
Feeder Mouse, Denmark, 2016
Unknown Animal, Lithuania, 2016

Washed-Up Calf Corpse, Israel, 2018

PREFACE: *Captivated by 'Captive'*

I first came across the work of Jo-Anne McArthur in December 2016 when I was given a copy of her first book, *We Animals,* as a Christmas present. Immediately, I was struck by the power of her visual images. However, it was not until September 2017 when I acquired a copy of her second book, *Captive,* that her images began to take root in my imagination.

I was totally unprepared for the impact that Jo-Anne's images in *Captive* would have on me. Nor was I prepared for the poetic form that presented itself to me as I began to try and write a response to them. As with writing any series of poems, once one has written a certain number they begin to come, if not fully formed, then at least with a family likeness. So it was with the *Zoospeak* poems.

In hindsight, I could say that it was my intention from the start that my use of the present tense, the first-person pronoun and repetition would mirror the symptoms of zoochosis in the various animals - pacing, walking in tight circles, rocking, swaying and, at times, self-harming. However, this was not the case. All I wanted to do was to get the words down - words which, I hoped, would do justice to the power of the visual images with which I had been confronted.

The writing process consisted of my trawling initially through the pages of *Captive* and then through Jo-Anne's *We Animals* site, allowing whichever image leapt out at me to be the subject of that day's writing.

It is certainly now both my hope and my intention that the form of the poems, juxtaposed as they are in this collection with the photographs that gave birth to them, does in some way underline the monotony and mental stress which animals in captivity without doubt experience.

I would like to take the opportunity to thank Jo-Anne McArthur for her photographs, Dave Rogers for his unstinting work in putting together this book, and my family for their support throughout the writing of the poems.

Gordon Meade
Upper Largo, 2019.

Foreword by Jo-Anne McArthur

Moving through the landscape of Gordon Meade's poetry, I stumble and pause over the brutality of his quiet observations as though I've been wounded by a bullet, or by love. I pause to catch my breath as the consideration of what these others may have felt and understood of their world sinks in.

Art imitates life here in repetition, mimicking the unhurried pace of the captive experience. I became uncertain as to whether Gordon was peeling away layers or adding them. I think it's both. He's removing our blinders and adding ideas and dimensions. The work is unexpected, and so complimentary to the images. Where my images might at first glance fail to illuminate the shadows, Gordon's words complete the task.

Gordon's is the careful work of time spent in consideration of itself and its subject matter. The result is as detailed as it is solemn. Like Philip Glass' symphonic pacing, *Zoospeak*'s cadence unfolds and sears. Ultimately, we are ushered to face the bear. The fox. The whale. The fish. It is raw. It is stark.

I had not noticed that one of the painted flamingos looked bored, and just one was preparing to fly. Thank you for looking deeply, Gordon.

Gordon's captive animals are begging to be seen and not forgotten at the bottoms of our bowls, and our quarries.

Moving from one exhibit to the next, we look at them. We throw coins. The turtle knows our wishes are not for her. The cat is dreaming of not being like any other cat.

We look but we don't see.

They look back at us. *You are no longer what I would call a human being.* Because we don't share a language, they cannot tell us that their crisis is our crisis. And so, Gordon does.

We are not regular! they cry out. They would be among the billions of us who contribute to the living tapestry of the world if they could. But they can only contribute through a glass darkly, rendered shadows in our constructs.

My photos brighten the glass. Gordon polishes it.

A dolphin is the focus of your attention for as long as you are here.

We are here. Gordon and I, and others.

And we are not going anywhere.

Chapeau, Gordon Meade.

We polish an animal mirror to look for ourselves.
- Donna Haraway

A Deer in the City, USA, 2005

Of course, I am not a real deer.
All I am is the stuffed head of a deer
being carried through the city.

Of course, I am not a real deer.
All I am is the stuffed head of a deer
being carried through the city
streets in the arms of a human.

Of course, I am not a real deer.
All I am is the stuffed head of a deer
being carried through the city
streets in the arms of a human.
Neither you, nor I, know why.

Of course, I am not a real deer.
All I am is the stuffed head of a deer
being carried through the city
streets in the arms of a human.
Neither you, nor I, know why
but, perhaps, that is not the point.

Of course, I am not a real deer.
All I am is the stuffed head of a deer
being carried through the city
streets in the arms of a human.
Neither you, nor I, know why
but, perhaps, that is not the point;
the human, that is carrying me, is.

Of course, I am not a real deer.
All I am is the stuffed head of a deer
being carried through the city
streets in the arms of a human.
Neither you, nor I, know why
but, perhaps, that is not the point.
The human, that is carrying me, is
staring straight into the camera.

Of course, I am not a real deer.
All I am is the stuffed head of a deer
being carried through the city
streets in the arms of a human.
Neither you, nor I, know why
but, perhaps, that is not the point.
The human, that is carrying me, is
staring straight into the camera,
and my glass eyes are fixed on her.

Part One
2008

The only creature on Earth whose natural habitat is a zoo is the zookeeper.
- Robert Brault

Bald Eagle, Canada, 2008

I am gazing over
the top of a Douglas Fir into
a source of fresh water.

I am gazing over
the top of a Douglas Fir into
a source of fresh water
which appears to be nothing.

I am gazing over
the top of a Douglas Fir into
a source of fresh water
which appears to be nothing
more than a litre or two.

I am gazing over
the top of a Douglas Fir into
a source of fresh water
which appears to be nothing
more than a litre or two
poured into a plastic bowl.

I am gazing over
the top of a Douglas Fir into
a source of fresh water
which appears to be nothing
more than a litre or two
poured into a plastic bowl.
There are no Sockeye in it.

I am gazing over
the top of a Douglas Fir into
a source of fresh water
which appears to be nothing
more than a litre or two
poured into a plastic bowl.
There are no Sockeye in it,
and the Douglas Fir is little.

I am gazing over
the top of a Douglas Fir into
a source of fresh water
which appears to be nothing
more than a litre or two
poured into a plastic bowl.
There are no Sockeye in it,
and the Douglas Fir is little
more than a stump.

Mata Mata Turtle, Thailand, 2008

I am trying to hide
at the bottom of a pool of water
but the water is clear.

I am trying to hide
at the bottom of a pool of water
but the water is clear
so that the people can see.

I am trying to hide
at the bottom of a pool of water
but the water is clear
so that the people can see
both myself and the money.

I am trying to hide
at the bottom of a pool of water
but the water is clear
so that the people can see
both myself and the money
they are throwing into it.

I am trying to hide
at the bottom of a pool of water
but the water is clear
so that the people can see
both myself and the money
they are throwing into it
in order to make wishes.

I am trying to hide
at the bottom of a pool of water
but the water is clear
so that the people can see
both myself and the money
they are throwing into it
in order to make wishes.
Once they are made they leave.

I am trying to hide
at the bottom of a pool of water
but the water is clear
so that the people can see
both myself and the money
they are throwing into it
in order to make wishes.
Once they are made they leave,
with none of them for me.

American White Pelican, Canada, 2008

It looks to all intents
and purposes that I am
in a room and not a cage.

It looks to all intents
and purposes that I am
in a room and not a cage.
There is a sealed off light switch.

It looks to all intents
and purposes that I am
in a room and not a cage.
There is a sealed off light switch
and an unpainted rectangle.

It looks to all intents
and purposes that I am
in a room and not a cage.
There is a sealed off light switch
and an unpainted rectangle
on one of the walls.

It looks to all intents
and purposes that I am
in a room and not a cage.
There is a sealed off light switch
and an unpainted rectangle
on one of the walls
where a radiator had been.

It looks to all intents
and purposes that I am
in a room and not a cage.
There is a sealed off light switch
and an unpainted rectangle
on one of the walls
where a radiator had been.
There is a bale of straw.

It looks to all intents
and purposes that I am
in a room and not a cage.
There is a sealed off light switch
and an unpainted rectangle
on one of the walls
where a radiator had been.
There is a bale of straw,
but no sign of fish at all.

Malayan Sun Bear, Thailand, 2008

I am just one of the ghosts
that you are likely to see here
if you are willing to look.

I am just one of the ghosts
that you are likely to see here
if you are willing to look
past the sheet of glass.

I am just one of the ghosts
that you are likely to see here
if you are willing to look
past the sheet of glass
that separates us – I have.

I am just one of the ghosts
that you are likely to see here
if you are willing to look
past the sheet of glass
that separates us. I have
raised my right paw.

I am just one of the ghosts
that you are likely to see here
if you are willing to look
past the sheet of glass
that separates us. I have
raised my right paw
and placed it against the pane.

I am just one of the ghosts
that you are likely to see here
if you are willing to look
past the sheet of glass
that separates us. I have
raised my right paw
and placed it against the pane.
Look into my eyes, my gaze.

I am just one of the ghosts
that you are likely to see here
if you are willing to look
past the sheet of glass
that separates us. I have
raised my right paw
and placed it against the pane.
Look into my eyes. My gaze
can cut right through it.

Red Panda, Canada, 2008

There are only so many times
that you can walk upon the same patch
of snow before it turns to solid ice.

There are only so many times
that you can walk upon the same patch
of snow before it turns to solid ice
or melts; I have walked that path.

There are only so many times
that you can walk upon the same patch
of snow before it turns to solid ice
or melts. I have walked that path
too many times; of course, I have.

There are only so many times
that you can walk upon the same patch
of snow before it turns to solid icc
or melts. I have walked that path
too many times. Of course, I have
access to a slightly higher plane.

There are only so many times
that you can walk upon the same patch
of snow before it turns to solid ice
or melts. I have walked that path
too many times. Of course, I have
access to a slightly higher plane,
from where I am able to look.

There are only so many times
that you can walk upon the same patch
of snow before it turns to solid ice
or melts. I have walked that path
too many times. Of course, I have
access to a slightly higher plane,
from where I am able to look
into another section of the zoo.

There are only so many times
that you can walk upon the same patch
of snow before it turns to solid ice
or melts. I have walked that path
too many times. Of course, I have
access to a slightly higher plane,
from where I am able to look
into another section of the zoo;
the one the humans call *Eurasia*.

Brown Bear, Germany, 2008

I am aware of what you are
and I am also aware of what you are
thinking. You are a human being.

I am aware of what you are
and I am also aware of what you are
thinking. You are a human being
and you are thinking I am something else.

I am aware of what you are
and I am also aware of what you are
thinking. You are a human being
and you are thinking I am something else
put here for your entertainment.

I am aware of what you are
and I am also aware of what you are
thinking. You are a human being
and you are thinking I am something else
put here for your entertainment,
that makes it easier for you to ignore me.

I am aware of what you are
and I am also aware of what you are
thinking. You are a human being
and you are thinking I am something else
put here for your entertainment.
That makes it easier for you to ignore me
and the wire mesh that surrounds me.

I am aware of what you are
and I am also aware of what you are
thinking. You are a human being
and you are thinking I am something else
put here for your entertainment.
That makes it easier for you to ignore me
and the wire mesh that surrounds me;
the wire mesh that separates us.

I am aware of what you are
and I am also aware of what you are
thinking. You are a human being
and you are thinking I am something else
put here for your entertainment.
That makes it easier for you to ignore me
and the wire mesh that surrounds me;
the wire mesh that separates us,
and your way of thinking from mine.

Polar Bear, Canada, 2008

It is hard for you to tell
whether or not I am praying
for snow or just staring.

It is hard for you to tell
whether or not I am praying
for snow or just staring
at an electric fence.

It is hard for you to tell
whether or not I am praying
for snow or just staring
at an electric fence;
and it is hard for me too.

It is hard for you to tell
whether or not I am praying
for snow or just staring
at an electric fence;
and it is hard for me too,
as there is no snow.

It is hard for you to tell
whether or not I am praying
for snow or just staring
at an electric fence;
and it is hard for me too,
as there is no snow.
I wonder what it was.

It is hard for you to tell
whether or not I am praying
for snow or just staring
at an electric fence;
and it is hard for me too,
as there is no snow.
I wonder what it was
that shocked me the most.

It is hard for you to tell
whether or not I am praying
for snow or just staring
at an electric fence;
and it is hard for me too,
as there is no snow.
I wonder what it was
that shocked me the most,
the lack of snow or the fence.

South American Sea Lion, Cuba, 2008

It looks as if I am going
to be a bit overlooked
in my solitary confinement.

It looks as if I am going
to be a bit overlooked
in my solitary confinement;
concrete flooring and metal railings.

It looks as if I am going
to be a bit overlooked
in my solitary confinement;
concrete flooring and metal railings,
dodgy looking water and high-rise flats.

It looks as if I am going
to be a bit overlooked
in my solitary confinement;
concrete flooring and metal railings,
dodgy looking water and high-rise flats.
This is not what I was used to in the wild.

It looks as if I am going
to be a bit overlooked
in my solitary confinement;
concrete flooring and metal railings,
dodgy looking water and high-rise flats.
This is not what I was used to in the wild;
open water and secluded beaches.

It looks as if I am going
to be a bit overlooked
in my solitary confinement;
concrete flooring and metal railings,
dodgy looking water and high-rise flats.
This is not what I was used to in the wild;
open water and secluded beaches.
On land, I was a member of a colony.

It looks as if I am going
to be a bit overlooked
in my solitary confinement;
concrete flooring and metal railings,
dodgy looking water and high-rise flats.
This is not what I was used to in the wild;
open water and secluded beaches.
On land, I was a member of a colony.
In the sea, I helped to make a raft.

Cougar, Canada, 2008

It looks as if I might be
just like any other cat,
sprawled out on the floor.

It looks as if I might be
just like any other cat,
sprawled out on the floor
of someone else's living-room.

It looks as if I might be
just like any other cat,
sprawled out on the floor
of someone else's living-room.
The truth is, though, I am not.

It looks as if I might be
just like any other cat,
sprawled out on the floor
of someone else's living-room.
The truth is, though, I am not.
I am a cougar lying on the floor.

It looks as if I might be
just like any other cat,
sprawled out on the floor
of someone else's living-room.
The truth is, though, I am not.
I am a cougar lying on the floor
of a cage overgrown with weeds.

It looks as if I might be
just like any other cat,
sprawled out on the floor
of someone else's living-room.
The truth is, though, I am not.
I am a cougar lying on the floor
of a cage overgrown with weeds;
dreaming of not being like any other cat.

It looks as if I might be
just like any other cat,
sprawled out on the floor
of someone else's living-room.
The truth is, though, I am not.
I am a cougar lying on the floor
of a cage overgrown with weeds;
dreaming of not being like any other cat;
just dreaming of being myself, and free.

American Flamingos, Canada, 2008

There are five of us here,
gathered around a feeding
station, in front of a mural.

There are five of us here,
gathered around a feeding
station, in front of a mural
on which are painted five more.

There are five of us here,
gathered around a feeding
station, in front of a mural
on which are painted five more
of us in different poses.

There are five of us here,
gathered around a feeding
station, in front of a mural
on which are painted five more
of us in different poses;
one drinking, another preening.

There are five of us here,
gathered around a feeding
station, in front of a mural
on which are painted five more
of us in different poses;
one drinking, another preening,
one looking as bored as we are.

There are five of us here,
gathered around a feeding
station, in front of a mural
on which are painted five more
of us in different poses;
one drinking, another preening,
one looking as bored as we are,
another partly hidden by foliage.

There are five of us here,
gathered around a feeding
station, in front of a mural
on which are painted five more
of us in different poses;
one drinking, another preening,
one looking as bored as we are,
another partly hidden by foliage,
and one, just one, preparing to fly.

Burmese Python, Canada, 2008

This is a fantastic set up and I am
so very proud to be a part of it. In fact, I am
the only living thing in this scenario.

This is a fantastic set up and I am
so very proud to be a part of it. In fact, I am
the only living thing in this scenario
that the camera has managed to capture.

This is a fantastic set up and I am
so very proud to be a part of it. In fact, I am
the only living thing in this scenario
that the camera has managed to capture.
I may look still but I am still alive. I am a circle.

This is a fantastic set up and I am
so very proud to be a part of it. In fact, I am
the only living thing in this scenario
that the camera has managed to capture.
I may look still but I am still alive. I am a circle
of flesh and blood against a backdrop of straw.

This is a fantastic set up and I am
so very proud to be a part of it. In fact, I am
the only living thing in this scenario
that the camera has managed to capture.
I may look still but I am still alive. I am a circle
of flesh and blood set against a backdrop of straw.
You cannot see it, but I am still breathing.

This is a fantastic set up and I am
so very proud to be a part of it. In fact, I am
the only living thing in this scenario
that the camera has managed to capture.
I may look still but I am still alive. I am a circle
of flesh and blood set against a backdrop of straw.
You cannot see it, but I am still breathing.
You cannot hear it, but the straw is rustling.

This is a fantastic set up and I am
so very proud to be a part of it. In fact, I am
the only living thing in this scenario
that the camera has managed to capture.
I may look still but I am still alive. I am a circle
of flesh and blood set against a backdrop of straw.
You cannot see it, but I am still breathing.
You cannot hear it, but the straw is rustling
underneath the weight of my coils.

Minnow, Cuba, 2008

*The fish was motionless, and I told the woman that I thought he
was dying. "No," she replied. "It's been like that for two years."*

This is what happens
during the early stages
of awakening. Things begin.

This is what happens
during the early stages
of awakening. Things begin
to stop; almost everything.

This is what happens
during the early stages
of awakening. Things begin
to stop. Almost everything
grinds to a halt - I have.

This is what happens
during the early stages
of awakening. Things begin
to stop. Almost everything
grinds to a halt. I have
been trying to awaken.

This is what happens
during the early stages
of awakening. Things begin
to stop. Almost everything
grinds to a halt. I have
been trying to awaken
now for almost two years.

This is what happens
during the early stages
of awakening. Things begin
to stop. Almost everything
grinds to a halt. I have
been trying to awaken
now for almost two years.
Look in to my eyes.

This is what happens
during the early stages
of awakening. Things begin
to stop. Almost everything
grinds to a halt. I have
been trying to awaken
now for almost two years.
Look in to my eyes;
are they alive or dead?

Part Two
2009 - 2015

Animals can communicate quite well. And generally speaking, they are ignored.
- Alice Walker

Spotted Hyena, Cameroon, 2009

Surely mine must be one
of those stares you simply can't deny;
the focussed/unfocussed sort.

Surely mine must be one
of those stares you simply can't deny;
the focussed/unfocussed sort
of look into the middle distance.

Surely mine must be one
of those stares you simply can't deny;
the focussed/unfocussed sort
of look into the middle distance
above the heads of all the passers-by.

Surely mine must be one
of those stares you simply can't deny;
the focussed/unfocussed sort
of look into the middle distance
above the heads of all the passers-by;
with neither they, nor I, aware.

Surely mine must be one
of those stares you simply can't deny;
the focussed/unfocussed sort
of look into the middle distance
above the heads of all the passers-by;
with neither they, nor I, aware
of what it is we could be sharing.

Surely mine must be one
of those stares you simply can't deny;
the focussed/unfocussed sort
of look into the middle distance
above the heads of all the passers-by;
with neither they, nor I, aware
of what it is we could be sharing;
the kind of gaze that might be passed.

Surely mine must be one
of those stares you simply can't deny;
the focussed/unfocussed sort
of look into the middle distance
above the heads of all the passers-by;
with neither they, nor I, aware
of what it is we could be sharing;
the kind of gaze that might be passed
between a jailbird and his screw.

Humboldt Penguin, Thailand, 2009

What was once being a part
of a cast of thousands, is now my own
reflection in a wall of glass.

What was once being a part
of a cast of thousands, is now my own
reflection in a wall of glass;
that was once a backdrop of islands.

What was once being a part
of a cast of thousands, is now my own
reflection in a wall of glass.
What was once a backdrop of islands,
is now a diorama of tropical plants.

What was once being a part
of a cast of thousands, is now my own
reflection in a wall of glass.
What was once a backdrop of islands,
is now a diorama of tropical plants;
that was once a dive into the South Pacific.

What was once being a part
of a cast of thousands, is now my own
reflection in a wall of glass.
What was once a backdrop of islands,
is now a diorama of tropical plants.
What was once a dive into the South Pacific,
is now a paddle in a man-made pool.

What was once being a part
of a cast of thousands, is now my own
reflection in a wall of glass.
What was once a backdrop of islands,
is now a diorama of tropical plants.
What was once a dive into the South Pacific,
is now a paddle in a man-made pool.
What was once, is now no longer.

What was once being a part
of a cast of thousands, is now my own
reflection in a wall of glass.
What was once a backdrop of islands,
is now a diorama of tropical plants.
What was once a dive into the South Pacific,
is now a paddle in a man-made pool.
What was once, is now no longer;
what remains, no more than what it is.

Tiger Temple, Thailand, 2009

We did not come to this temple
by design. We just stumbled upon it.
Nor did we ask to be cared for.

We did not come to this temple
by design. We just stumbled upon it.
Nor did we ask to be cared for
by the Buddhist monks who live here.

We did not come to this temple
by design. We just stumbled upon it.
Nor did we ask to be cared for
by the Buddhist monks who live here.
True, we are fed and watered by them.

We did not come to this temple
by design. We just stumbled upon it.
Nor did we ask to be cared for
by the Buddhist monks who live here.
True, we are fed and watered by them,
but we are also led around in chains.

We did not come to this temple
by design. We just stumbled upon it.
Nor did we ask to be cared for
by the Buddhist monks who live here.
True, we are fed and watered by them,
but we are also led around in chains.
Maybe you will remember this.

We did not come to this temple
by design. We just stumbled upon it.
Nor did we ask to be cared for
by the Buddhist monks who live here.
True, we are fed and watered by them,
but we are also led around in chains.
Maybe you will remember this
as you pose with us for photographs.

We did not come to this temple
by design. We just stumbled upon it.
Nor did we ask to be cared for
by the Buddhist monks who live here.
True, we are fed and watered by them,
but we are also led around in chains.
Maybe you will remember this
as you pose with us for photographs
at the bottom of a nearby quarry.

Silver Fox, Sweden, 2010

I think you have, as far
as is possible, given the present
circumstances, definitely succeeded.

I think you have, as far
as is possible, given the present
circumstances, definitely succeeded
in capturing my best side.

I think you have, as far
as is possible, given the present
circumstances, definitely succeeded
in capturing my best side,
my stoic pose, beyond the bars.

I think you have, as far
as is possible, given the present
circumstances, definitely succeeded
in capturing my best side,
my stoic pose. Beyond the bars
of my cage, the night air bristles.

I think you have, as far
as is possible, given the present
circumstances, definitely succeeded
in capturing my best side,
my stoic pose. Beyond the bars
of my cage, the night air bristles
but I am no longer party to that.

I think you have, as far
as is possible, given the present
circumstances, definitely succeeded
in capturing my best side,
my stoic pose. Beyond the bars
of my cage, the night air bristles
but I am no longer party to that.
My gaze remains turned inward.

I think you have, as far
as is possible, given the present
circumstances, definitely succeeded
in capturing my best side,
my stoic pose. Beyond the bars
of my cage, the night air bristles
but I am no longer party to that.
My gaze remains turned inward.
My eyes have seen too much.

Walrus, USA, 2011

I am so happy to have
been made a part of your work
of art. It is so clever.

I am so happy to have
been made a part of your work
of art. It is so clever
what you have managed.

I am so happy to have
been made a part of your work
of art. It is so clever
what you have managed
to do; been able to capture.

I am so happy to have
been made a part of your work
of art. It is so clever
what you have managed
to do; been able to capture
my existence as it is.

I am so happy to have
been made a part of your work
of art. It is so clever
what you have managed
to do; been able to capture
my existence as it is
now and, also, the world.

I am so happy to have
been made a part of your work
of art. It is so clever
what you have managed
to do; been able to capture
my existence as it is
now and, also, the world
from where I came.

I am so happy to have
been made a part of your work
of art. It is so clever
what you have managed
to do; been able to capture
my existence as it is
now and, also, the world
from where I came;
and all of it in a single shot.

Macaque, Laos, 2011

Am I still in shock? Or am I,
by now, in mourning? Or am I
just sitting, waiting for the body?

Am I still in shock? Or am I,
by now, in mourning? Or am I
just sitting, waiting for the body
of the dead to be taken away?

Am I still in shock? Or am I,
by now, in mourning? Or am I
just sitting, waiting for the body
of the dead to be taken away
from me? I am holding myself.

Am I still in shock? Or am I,
by now, in mourning? Or am I
just sitting, waiting for the body
of the dead to be taken away
from me? I am holding myself
closely as there is no-one else here.

Am I still in shock? Or am I,
by now, in mourning? Or am I
just sitting, waiting for the body
of the dead to be taken away
from me? I am holding myself
closely as there is no-one else here
who is either willing or able to do it.

Am I still in shock? Or am I,
by now, in mourning? Or am I
just sitting, waiting for the body
of the dead to be taken away
from me? I am holding myself
closely as there is no-one else here
who is either willing or able to do it
for me. This is what death looks like.

Am I still in shock? Or am I,
by now, in mourning? Or am I
just sitting, waiting for the body
of the dead to be taken away
from me? I am holding myself
closely as there is no-one else here
who is either willing or able to do it
for me. This is what death looks like
in a cage at a breeding facility in Laos.

Bottle-Nosed Dolphin, USA, 2012

Here, there is a semblance
of caring, the illusion of freedom,
and a yearning for love.

Here, there is a semblance
of caring, the illusion of freedom,
and a yearning for love.
I am the object of your gaze.

Here, there is a semblance
of caring, the illusion of freedom,
and a yearning for love.
I am the object of your gaze.
I am the focus of your attention.

Here, there is a semblance
of caring, the illusion of freedom,
and a yearning for love.
I am the object of your gaze.
I am the focus of your attention
for as long as you are here.

Here, there is a semblance
of caring, the illusion of freedom,
and a yearning for love.
I am the object of your gaze.
I am the focus of your attention.
For as long as you are here
almost anything seems possible.

Here, there is a semblance
of caring, the illusion of freedom,
and a yearning for love.
I am the object of your gaze.
I am the focus of your attention.
For as long as you are here
almost anything seems possible;
leaving, very little remains.

Here, there is a semblance
of caring, the illusion of freedom,
and a yearning for love.
I am the object of your gaze.
I am the focus of your attention.
For as long as you are here
almost anything seems possible;
leaving, very little remains –
for you, a memory; me, a pen.

Sea Lion, Europe, 2012

I am standing
behind a podium
somewhere in Europe.

I am standing
behind a podium
somewhere in Europe
looking as if I might be.

I am standing
behind a podium
somewhere in Europe
looking as if I might be
about to read.

I am standing
behind a podium
somewhere in Europe
looking as if I might be
about to read
a couple of poems.

I am standing
behind a podium
somewhere in Europe
looking as if I might be
about to read
a couple of poems
from the pages of a book.

I am standing
behind a podium
somewhere in Europe
looking as if I might be
about to read
a couple of poems
from the pages of a book,
but I am a sea lion.

I am standing
behind a podium
somewhere in Europe
looking as if I might be
about to read
a couple of poems
from the pages of a book,
but I am a sea lion,
and sea lions can't read.

Sawfish, Australia, 2013

It is hardly my fault
that, from a certain angle,
my nostrils look like eyes.

It is hardly my fault
that, from a certain angle,
my nostrils look like eyes;
nor that my mouth is set.

It is hardly my fault
that, from a certain angle,
my nostrils look like eyes,
nor that my mouth is set
in a semi-permanent grin.

It is hardly my fault
that, from a certain angle,
my nostrils look like eyes,
nor that my mouth is set
in a semi-permanent grin.
It is hardly my fault.

It is hardly my fault
that, from a certain angle,
my nostrils look like eyes;
nor that my mouth is set
in a semi-permanent grin.
It is hardly my fault
that all you want to do is take.

It is hardly my fault
that, from a certain angle,
my nostrils look like eyes;
nor that my mouth is set
in a semi-permanent grin.
It is hardly my fault
that all you want to do is take
a snap of me and post it.

It is hardly my fault
that, from a certain angle,
my nostrils look like eyes;
nor that my mouth is set
in a semi-permanent grin.
It is hardly my fault
that all you want to do is take
a snap of me and post it
on Instagram for all to see.

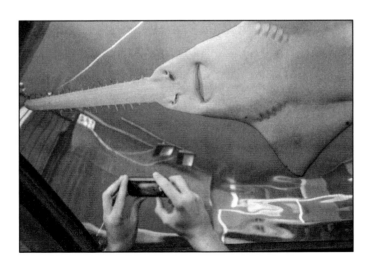

Orca, Canada, 2013

In the wild, I would normally cover
just under one hundred miles a day;
just think of that compared to this.

In the wild, I would normally cover
just under one hundred miles a day;
just think of that compared to this.
In the wild, I would normally swim.

In the wild, I would normally cover
just under one hundred miles a day;
just think of that compared to this.
In the wild, I would normally swim
in clean water; just think of that.

In the wild, I would normally cover
just under one hundred miles a day;
just think of that compared to this.
In the wild, I would normally swim
in clean water; just think of that
compared to this. In the wild, I would.

In the wild, I would normally cover
just under one hundred miles a day;
just think of that compared to this.
In the wild, I would normally swim
in clean water; just think of that
compared to this. In the wild, I would
normally be a member of a pod.

In the wild, I would normally cover
just under one hundred miles a day;
just think of that compared to this.
In the wild, I would normally swim
in clean water; just think of that
compared to this. In the wild, I would
normally be a member of a pod;
just think of that compared to this.

In the wild, I would normally cover
just under one hundred miles a day;
just think of that compared to this.
In the wild, I would normally swim
in clean water; just think of that
compared to this. In the wild, I would
normally be a member of a pod;
just think of that compared to this.
In the wild, I would normally be free.

Rocky and the American Flag, USA, 2014

Isn't this ace, I mean, amn't I
just the perfect subject for a shot?
Just look at what you've got.

Isn't this ace, I mean, amn't I
just the perfect subject for a shot?
Just look at what you've got -
an American flag tacked to the back.

Isn't this ace, I mean, amn't I
just the perfect subject for a shot?
Just look at what you've got -
an American flag tacked to the back
of a makeshift screen, and I, myself.

Isn't this ace, I mean, amn't I
just the perfect subject for a shot?
Just look at what you've got -
an American flag tacked to the back
of a makeshift screen, and I, myself,
doing my damnedest to slither underneath.

Isn't this ace, I mean, amn't I
just the perfect subject for a shot?
Just look at what you've got -
an American flag tacked to the back
of a makeshift screen, and I, myself,
doing my damnedest to slither underneath,
and almost succeeding, snarling and growling.

Isn't this ace, I mean, amn't I
just the perfect subject for a shot?
Just look at what you've got -
an American flag tacked to the back
of a makeshift screen, and I, myself,
doing my damnedest to slither underneath,
and almost succeeding, snarling and growling,
if not quite heading for the dream; the dream.

Isn't this ace, I mean, amn't I
just the perfect subject for a shot?
Just look at what you've got -
an American flag tacked to the back
of a makeshift screen, and I, myself,
doing my damnedest to slither underneath,
and almost succeeding, snarling and growling,
if not quite heading for the dream. The dream
that nearly all of us have, by now, forgotten.

Hyena, Europe, 2015

My ears are intact.
There have been no chunks
taken out of them.

My ears are intact.
There have been no chunks
taken out of them.
My ears are intact.

My ears are intact.
There have been no chunks
taken out of them.
My ears are intact,
as is my snout - no scars.

My ears are intact.
There have been no chunks
taken out of them.
My ears are intact,
as is my snout; no scars
visible along its length.

My ears are intact.
There have been no chunks
taken out of them.
My ears are intact,
as is my snout; no scars
visible along its length.
My ears are intact.

My ears are intact.
There have been no chunks
taken out of them.
My ears are intact,
as is my snout; no scars
visible along its length.
My ears are intact.
I hear every word you say.

My ears are intact.
There have been no chunks
taken out of them.
My ears are intact,
as is my snout; no scars
visible along its length.
My ears are intact.
I hear every word you say,
but my eyes are dead.

Part Three
2016 (i)

When was the last time you asked a wild nonhuman how he or she was doing? When was the last time you even considered what life might be like for one of these others? When was the last time you cared?
- Derrick Jensen

Brown Bear, Denmark, 2016

I am looking
at a statue of myself
carved out of wood.

I am looking
at a statue of myself
carved out of wood
and wondering.

I am looking
at a statue of myself
carved out of wood
and wondering
which of us is real.

I am looking
at a statue of myself
carved out of wood
and wondering
which of us is real,
which of us is free.

I am looking
at a statue of myself
carved out of wood
and wondering
which of us is real,
which of us is free,
which of us is nothing.

I am looking
at a statue of myself
carved out of wood
and wondering
which of us is real,
which of us is free,
which of us is nothing
but a representation.

I am looking
at a statue of myself
carved out of wood
and wondering
which of us is real,
which of us is free,
which of us is nothing
but a representation;
which of us is me.

Red Fox, Lithuania, 2016

I am lying
on the concrete
floor of my cage.

I am lying
on the concrete
floor of my cage
next to a drain.

I am lying
on the concrete
floor of my cage
next to a drain
and I am dreaming.

I am lying
on the concrete
floor of my cage
next to a drain
and I am dreaming
of the truth.

I am lying
on the concrete
floor of my cage
next to a drain
and I am dreaming
of the truth
that is the wild.

I am lying
on the concrete
floor of my cage
next to a drain
and I am dreaming
of the truth
that is the wild
which they cannot.

I am lying
on the concrete
floor of my cage
next to a drain
and I am dreaming
of the truth
that is the wild
which they cannot
take away from me.

Orangutan, Denmark, 2016

I have no interest
in the terracotta tiles that pave
the floor of my cage.

I have no interest
in the terracotta tiles that pave
the floor of my cage.
I have no interest at all.

I have no interest
in the terracotta tiles that pave
the floor of my cage.
I have no interest at all
in any of the toys I have.

I have no interest
in the terracotta tiles that pave
the floor of my cage.
I have no interest at all
in any of the toys I have
been given to play with.

I have no interest
in the terracotta tiles that pave
the floor of my cage.
I have no interest at all
in any of the toys I have
been given to play with.
My interest lies in all that is.

I have no interest
in the terracotta tiles that pave
the floor of my cage.
I have no interest at all
in any of the toys I have
been given to play with.
My interest lies in all that is
left of me – I am engrossed.

I have no interest
in the terracotta tiles that pave
the floor of my cage.
I have no interest at all
in any of the toys I have
been given to play with.
My interest lies in all that is
left of me. I am engrossed
in examining myself.

Amur Leopard, France, 2016

Beauty is truth, truth beauty.
- John Keats

It looks as if I take
too good a shot
to be taken seriously.

It looks as if I take
too good a shot
to be taken seriously
here, in France.

It looks as if I take
too good a shot
to be taken seriously.
Here, in France,
beauty is not truth.

It looks as if I take
too good a shot
to be taken seriously.
Here, in France,
beauty is not truth,
and truth is nothing.

It looks as if I take
too good a shot
to be taken seriously.
Here, in France,
beauty is not truth,
and truth has nothing
to do with beauty.

It looks as if I take
too good a shot
to be taken seriously.
Here, in France,
beauty is not truth,
and truth has nothing
to do with beauty.
Beauty often hides.

It looks as if I take
too good a shot
to be taken seriously.
Here, in France,
beauty is not truth,
and truth has nothing
to do with beauty.
Beauty often hides
the pain of truth.

Asian Elephant, Slovenia, 2016

All I am asking is that you take
a good long look at where I am living;
a concrete box with a painting of a rain-forest.

All I am asking is that you take
a good long look at where I am living;
a concrete box with a painting of a rain-forest
daubed across two of its walls. There is also a door.

All I am asking is that you take
a good long look at where I am living;
a concrete box with a painting of a rain-forest
daubed across two of its walls. There is also a door
that opens out onto the rest of my enclosure.

All I am asking is that you take
a good long look at where I am living;
a concrete box with a painting of a rain-forest
daubed across two of its walls. There is also a door
that opens out onto the rest of my enclosure,
but this is my inner sanctum. This is my place.

All I am asking is that you take
a good long look at where I am living;
a concrete box with a painting of a rain-forest
daubed across two of its walls. There is also a door
that opens out onto the rest of my enclosure,
but this is my inner sanctum. This is my place
of rest. This is where I try to sleep.

All I am asking is that you take
a good long look at where I am living;
a concrete box with a painting of a rain-forest
daubed across two of its wall. There is also a door
that opens out onto the rest of my enclosure,
but this is my inner sanctum. This is my place
of rest. This is where I try to sleep,
and this is where, occasionally, I dream.

All I am asking is that you take
a good long look at where I am living;
a concrete box with a painting of a rain-forest
daubed across two of its walls. There is also a door
that opens out onto the rest of my enclosure,
but this is my inner sanctum. This is my place
of rest. This is where I try to sleep,
and this is where, occasionally, I dream;
a concrete box, a mural, and a door.

Snow Leopard, Lithuania, 2016

No snow, hardly
any leopard left,
and very little idea.

No snow, hardly
any leopard left,
and very little idea
as to where I might be.

No snow, hardly
any leopard left,
and very little idea
as to where I might be;
lots of metal and wood.

No snow, hardly
any leopard left,
and very little idea
as to where I might be;
lots of metal and wood
but not much else.

No snow, hardly
any leopard left,
and very little idea
as to where I might be;
lots of metal and wood
but not much else;
a pair of eyes staring.

No snow, hardly
any leopard left,
and very little idea
as to where I might be;
lots of metal and wood
but not much else;
a pair of eyes staring
at you through iron bars.

No snow, hardly
any leopard left,
and very little idea
as to where I might be;
lots of metal and wood
but not much else;
a pair of eyes staring
at you through iron bars;
reflecting nothing.

Chimpanzee, Denmark, 2016

There is a way in which,
had I chosen this sort of life myself,
it might well have been OK.

There is a way in which,
had I chosen this sort of life myself,
it might well have been OK.
It looks as if I am deep in thought.

There is a way in which,
had I chosen this sort of life myself,
it might well have been OK.
It looks as if I am deep in thought,
arms crossed, looking out a window.

There is a way in which,
had I chosen this sort of life myself,
it might well have been OK.
It looks as if I am deep in thought,
arms crossed, looking out a window
onto the world without a single care.

There is a way in which,
had I chosen this sort of life myself,
it might well have been OK.
It looks as if I am deep in thought,
arms crossed, looking out a window,
onto the world without a single care.
However, this is not the case.

There is a way in which,
had I chosen this sort of life myself,
it might well have been OK.
It looks as if I am deep in thought,
arms crossed, looking out a window,
onto the world without a single care.
However, this is not the case.
My choices were made for me.

There is a way in which,
had I chosen this sort of life myself,
it might well have been OK.
It looks as if I am deep in thought,
arms crossed, looking out a window,
onto the world without a single care.
However, this is not the case.
My choices were made for me,
by the likes of you, many years ago.

Leopards, Germany, 2016

In Norse mythology, Urda, Verdandi and Skuld
are the three Norns.

There are three of us in here,
housed in an enclosure no more than
the size of an average human living room.

There are three of us in here,
housed in an enclosure no more than
the size of an average human living room.
One of us is gazing at the crowds.

There are three of us in here,
housed in an enclosure no more than
the size of an average human living room.
One of us is gazing at the crowds,
another is turning to face the wall.

There are three of us in here,
housed in an enclosure no more than
the size of an average human living room.
One of us is gazing at the crowds,
another is turning to face the wall,
while the last of us is little more than a blur.

There are three of us in here,
housed in an enclosure no more than
the size of an average human living room.
One of us is gazing at the crowds,
another is turning to face the wall,
while the last of us is little more than a blur,
pacing back and forth behind the bars.

There are three of us in here,
housed in an enclosure no more than
the size of an average human living room.
One of us is gazing at the crowds,
another is turning to face the wall,
while the last of us is little more than a blur,
pacing back and forth behind the bars.
There are three of us housed in here.

There are three of us in here,
housed in an enclosure no more than
the size of an average human living room.
One of us is gazing at the crowds,
another is turning to face the wall,
while the last of us is little more than a blur,
pacing back and forth behind the bars.
There are three of us housed in here;
our names are Urda, Verdandi and Skuld.

Western Lowland Gorilla, Poland, 2016

There are bits of wood
that look like trees. There
are concrete walls.

There are bits of wood
that look like trees. There
are concrete walls
that look like stone.

There are bits of wood
that look like trees. There
are concrete walls
that look like stone.
There are two doorways.

There are bits of wood
that look like trees. There
are concrete walls
that look like stone.
There are two doorways;
one for in and one for out.

There are bits of wood
that look like trees. There
are concrete walls
that look like stone.
There are two doorways;
one for in and one for out
and, also, quite a lot of ropes.

There are bits of wood
that look like trees. There
are concrete walls
that look like stone.
There are two doorways;
one for in and one for out
and, also, quite a lot of ropes,
some of which are knotted.

There are bits of wood
that look like trees. There
are concrete walls
that look like stone.
There are two doorways;
one for in and one for out
and, also, quite a lot of ropes,
some of which are knotted
and some of which are not.

Brown Bear, Croatia, 2016

I used to be just fur, claws, snout, and skin.
But, now, thanks to you and your kind, I am
also, Perspex, metal, concrete, and stone.

I used to be just fur, claws, snout, and skin.
But, now, thanks to you and your kind, I am
also, Perspex, metal, concrete, and stone.
I have no way of knowing where I end.

I used to be just fur, claws, snout, and skin.
But, now, thanks to you and your kind, I am
also, Perspex, metal, concrete, and stone.
I have no way of knowing where I end
and the rest of the world begins; where?

I used to be just fur, claws, snout, and skin.
But, now, thanks to you and your kind, I am
also, Perspex, metal, concrete, and stone.
I have no way of knowing where I end
and the rest of the world begins; where
I begin and the rest of the world ceases.

I used to be just fur, claws, snout, and skin.
But, now, thanks to you and your kind, I am
also, Perspex, metal, concrete, and stone.
I have no way of knowing where I end
and the rest of the world begins; where
I begin and the rest of the world ceases
to exist. I am no more what you would call.

I used to be just fur, claws, snout, and skin.
But, now, thanks to you and your kind, I am
also, Perspex, metal, concrete, and stone.
I have no way of knowing where I end
and the rest of the world begins; where
I begin and the rest of the world ceases
to exist. I am no more what you would call
a 'proper' bear, in the same way as you are.

I used to be just fur, claws, snout, and skin.
But, now, thanks to you and your kind, I am
also, Perspex, metal, concrete, and stone.
I have no way of knowing where I end
and the rest of the world begins; where
I begin and the rest of the world ceases
to exist. I am no more what you would call
a 'proper' bear, in the same way as you are
no longer what I would call a human being.

Sand Tiger Shark, Canada, 2016

Mine is a portrait, not
a landscape and, also, a tad
surreal. I am a shadow.

Mine is a portrait, not
a landscape and, also, a tad
surreal. I am a shadow,
suspended overhead, moving.

Mine is a portrait, not
a landscape and, also, a tad
surreal. I am a shadow,
suspended overhead, moving
so slow as to be almost imperceptible.

Mine is a portrait, not
a landscape and, also, a tad
surreal. I am a shadow,
suspended overhead, moving
so slow as to be almost imperceptible.
You are in a tunnel underneath me.

Mine is a portrait, not
a landscape and, also, a tad
surreal. I am a shadow,
suspended overhead, moving
so slow as to be almost imperceptible.
You are in a tunnel underneath me,
and straining to look up at me.

Mine is a portrait, not
a landscape and, also, a tad
surreal. I am a shadow,
suspended overhead, moving
so slow as to be almost imperceptible.
You are in a tunnel underneath me,
and straining to look up at me,
so that you can take another snap.

Mine is a portrait, not
a landscape and, also, a tad
surreal. I am a shadow,
suspended overhead, moving
so slow as to be almost imperceptible.
You are in a tunnel underneath me,
and straining to look up at me,
so that you can take another snap.
I, however, am staring straight ahead.

Burrowing Owl, Denmark, 2016

Somehow, I have not managed to make it
underground. Instead, I am standing on a branch
attached to a sawn-off tree stump.

Somehow, I have not managed to make it
underground. Instead, I am standing on a branch
attached to a sawn-off tree stump.
There is not enough earth here for me.

Somehow, I have not managed to make it
underground. Instead, I am standing on a branch
attached to a sawn-off tree stump.
There is not enough earth here for me
to dig myself a burrow, nor enough sky.

Somehow, I have not managed to make it
underground. Instead, I am standing on a branch
attached to a sawn-off tree stump.
There is not enough earth here for me
to dig myself a burrow, nor enough sky
for me to open up my wings and fly.

Somehow, I have not managed to make it
underground. Instead, I am standing on a branch
attached to a sawn-off tree stump.
There is not enough earth here for me
to dig myself a burrow, nor enough sky
for me to open up my wings and fly;
all things having been considered.

Somehow, I have not managed to make it
underground. Instead, I am standing on a branch
attached to a sawn-off tree stump.
There is not enough earth here for me
to dig myself a burrow, nor enough sky
for me to open up my wings and fly.
All things having been considered,
what I could really do with is a bowl.

Somehow, I have not managed to make it
underground. Instead, I am standing on a branch
attached to a sawn-off tree stump.
There is not enough earth here for me
to dig myself a burrow, nor enough sky
for me to open up my wings and fly.
All things having been considered,
what I could really do with is a bowl
of water in which to drown my sorrows.

Part Four

2016 (ii)

One day we will know that all animals have a soul.
Hopefully, this knowledge does not come when it is
too late.
- Anthony Douglas Williams

Lynx, Denmark, 2016

Don't I just take
an amazing snapshot;
one eye, one ear.

Don't I just take
an amazing snapshot;
one eye, one ear,
and very little else.

Don't I just take
an amazing snapshot;
one eye, one ear,
and very little else,
apart from the darkness.

Don't I just take
an amazing snapshot;
one eye, one ear,
and very little else,
apart from the darkness
that is my cage.

Don't I just take
an amazing snapshot;
one eye, one ear,
and very little else,
apart from the darkness
that is my cage.
I have nothing to say.

Don't I just take
an amazing snapshot;
one eye, one ear,
and very little else,
apart from the darkness
that is my cage.
I have nothing to say.
My lips are sealed.

Don't I just take
an amazing snapshot;
one eye, one ear,
and very little else,
apart from the darkness
that is my cage.
I have nothing to say.
My lips are sealed.
I speak volumes.

White Tiger, France, 2016

Just like the proverbial pink
elephant, apart from the occasional
albino, I do not really exist.

Just like the proverbial pink
elephant, apart from the occasional
albino, I do not really exist
in the wild, just like those toy dogs.

Just like the proverbial pink
elephant, apart from the occasional
albino, I do not really exist
in the wild, just like those toy dogs
you cannot stop yourself from breeding.

Just like the proverbial pink
elephant, apart from the occasional
albino, I do not really exist
in the wild. Just like those toy dogs
you cannot stop yourself from breeding,
I, too, am a genetically modified model.

Just like the proverbial pink
elephant, apart from the occasional
albino, I do not really exist
in the wild. Just like those toy dogs
you cannot stop yourself from breeding,
I, too, am a genetically modified model
of myself; drained of my natural colour.

Just like the proverbial pink
elephant, apart from the occasional
albino, I do not really exist
in the wild. Just like those toy dogs
you cannot stop yourself from breeding,
I, too, am a genetically modified model
of myself; drained of my natural colour.
Apparently, that is my novelty value.

Just like the proverbial pink
elephant, apart from the occasional
albino, I do not really exist
in the wild. Just like those toy dogs
you cannot stop yourself from breeding,
I, too, am a genetically modified model
of myself. Drained of my natural colour,
apparently, it is my novelty value
that still pulls in the crowds.

Lion, Croatia, 2016

Nobody told me
that today was
World Animal Day.

Nobody told me
that today was
World Animal Day
and, so you see, I slept.

Nobody told me
that today was
World Animal Day
and, so you see, I slept
right through it.

Nobody told me
that today was
World Animal Day
and, so you see, I slept
right through it;
in spite of all the cameras.

Nobody told me
that today was
World Animal Day
and, so you see, I slept
right through it;
in spite of all the cameras;
in spite of all the crowds.

Nobody told me
that today was
World Animal Day
and, so you see, I slept
right through it;
in spite of all the cameras;
in spite of all the crowds;
in spite of all the headlines.

Nobody told me
that today was
World Animal Day
and, so you see, I slept
right through it;
in spite of all the cameras;
in spite of all the crowds;
in spite of all the headlines;
nobody told me.

Baltic Grey Seal, Lithuania, 2016

It is a sunny day. There are blue balloons
tied to the silver railings, and everyone is here,
dressed in their Sunday best. They are not.

It is a sunny day. There are blue balloons
tied to the silver railings, and everyone is here,
dressed in their Sunday best. They are not,
however, gathered together to celebrate.

It is a sunny day. There are blue balloons
tied to the silver railings, and everyone is here,
dressed in their Sunday best. They are not,
however, gathered together to celebrate
someone's birthday. Today marks the opening.

It is a sunny day. There are blue balloons
tied to the silver railings, and everyone is here,
dressed in their Sunday best. They are not,
however, gathered together to celebrate
someone's birthday. Today marks the opening
of my new enclosure. The water too is blue.

It is a sunny day. There are blue balloons
tied to the silver railings, and everyone is here,
dressed in their Sunday best. They are not,
however, gathered together to celebrate
someone's birthday. Today marks the opening
of my new enclosure. The water too is blue.
The rubber ring is red, but my skin is grey.

It is a sunny day. There are blue balloons
tied to the silver railings, and everyone is here,
dressed in their Sunday best. They are not,
however, gathered together to celebrate
someone's birthday. Today marks the opening
of my new enclosure. The water too is blue.
The rubber ring is red, but my skin is grey
just like the Baltic Sea in which I was born.

It is a sunny day. There are blue balloons
tied to the silver railings, and everyone is here,
dressed in their Sunday best. They are not,
however, gathered together to celebrate
someone's birthday. Today marks the opening
of my new enclosure. The water too is blue.
The rubber ring is red, but my skin is grey
just like the Baltic Sea in which I was born
and to which I will never be able to return.

California Sea Lion, Denmark, 2016

The Impossibility of Death in the Mind
of Someone Living – Damien Hirst

In spite of the obvious similarities,
I am not, nor, as far as I am aware,
have I ever been, a dead tiger shark.

In spite of the obvious similarities,
I am not, nor, as far as I am aware,
have I ever been, a dead tiger shark,
slowly decomposing in an art gallery.

In spite of the obvious similarities,
I am not, nor, as far as I am aware,
have I ever been, a dead tiger shark,
slowly decomposing in an art gallery
in England. Rather, I am a sea lion.

In spite of the obvious similarities,
I am not, nor, as far as I am aware,
have I ever been, a dead tiger shark,
slowly decomposing in an art gallery
in England. Rather, I am a sea lion,
housed alone in a zoo in Denmark.

In spite of the obvious similarities,
I am not, nor, as far as I am aware,
have I ever been, a dead tiger shark,
slowly decomposing in an art gallery
in England. Rather, I am a sea lion
housed alone in a zoo in Denmark;
with, occasionally, the idea of death.

In spite of the obvious similarities,
I am not, nor, as far as I am aware,
have I ever been, a dead tiger shark,
slowly decomposing in an art gallery
in England. Rather, I am a sea lion,
housed alone in a zoo in Denmark;
with, occasionally, the idea of death
uppermost in my mind; a shadow.

In spite of the obvious similarities,
I am not, nor, as far as I am aware,
have I ever been, a dead tiger shark,
slowly decomposing in an art gallery
in England. Rather, I am a sea lion
housed alone in a zoo in Denmark;
with, occasionally, the idea of death
uppermost in my mind; a shadow
sometimes; sometimes, a release.

Pileated Gibbon, France, 2016

As you come upon me, I am
seated, almost cross-legged,
with my arms folded; not quite.

As you come upon me, I am
seated, almost cross-legged,
with my arms folded. Not quite
the Full Lotus, but very nearly.

As you come upon me, I am
seated, almost cross-legged,
with my arms folded. Not quite
the Full Lotus, but very nearly
in the shape and form of one.

As you come upon me, I am
seated, almost cross-legged,
with my arms folded. Not quite
the Full Lotus, but very nearly
in the shape and form of one
of your spiritual icons; a Buddha.

As you come upon me, I am
seated, almost cross-legged,
with my arms folded. Not quite
the Full Lotus, but very nearly
in the shape and form of one
of your spiritual icons; a Buddha
in fur, with my eyes both open.

As you come upon me, I am
seated, almost cross-legged,
with my arms folded. Not quite
the Full Lotus, but very nearly
in the shape and form of one
of your spiritual icons; a Buddha
in fur, with my eyes both open
and closed, focussed and relaxed.

As you come upon me, I am
seated, almost cross-legged,
with my arms folded. Not quite
the Full Lotus, but very nearly
in the shape and form of one
of your spiritual icons; a Buddha
in fur, with my eyes both open
and closed, focussed and relaxed.
Here I am and, here, I am not.

Green Iguana, France, 2016

Is it not as if you have, somehow,
caught yourself looking down the wrong
end of a telescopic lens at a snapshot?

Is it not as if you have, somehow,
caught yourself looking down the wrong
end of a telescopic lens at a snapshot
of the past? After all, if nothing else, I have.

Is it not as if you have, somehow,
caught yourself looking down the wrong
end of a telescopic lens at a snapshot
of the past? After all, if nothing else, I have
always been one of your reptilian ancestors.

Is it not as if you have, somehow,
caught yourself looking down the wrong
end of a telescopic lens at a snapshot
of the past? After all, if nothing else, I have
always been one of your reptilian ancestors;
a living embodiment of the age of dinosaurs.

Is it not as if you have, somehow,
caught yourself looking down the wrong
end of a telescopic lens at a snapshot
of the past? After all, if nothing else, I have
always been one of your reptilian ancestors,
a living embodiment of the age of dinosaurs.
And I, too, cold-eyed and quizzical, am looking at you.

Is it not as if you have, somehow,
caught yourself looking down the wrong
end of a telescopic lens at a snapshot
of the past? After all, if nothing else, I have
always been one of your reptilian ancestors,
a living embodiment of the age of dinosaurs.
And I, too, cold-eyed and quizzical, am looking at you;
one of the representatives of our uncertain future.

Is it not as if you have, somehow,
caught yourself looking down the wrong
end of a telescopic lens at a snapshot
of the past? After all, if nothing else, I have
always been one of your reptilian ancestors,
a living embodiment of the age of dinosaurs.
And I, too, cold-eyed and quizzical, am looking at you;
one of the representatives of our uncertain future,
one to which either one of us might not belong.

Plains Buffalo, France, 2016

Who the hell are you
trying to kid? Definitely not me!
This is nothing like the plains.

Who the hell are you
trying to kid? Definitely not me!
This is nothing like the plains,
and I am not a regular buffalo.

Who the hell are you
trying to kid? Definitely not me!
This is nothing like the plains,
and I am not a regular buffalo.
For a start, I am surrounded by fences.

Who the hell are you
trying to kid? Definitely not me!
This is nothing like the plains,
and I am not a regular buffalo.
For a start, I am surrounded by fences,
and there is only one of me.

Who the hell are you
trying to kid? Definitely not me!
This is nothing like the plains,
and I am not a regular buffalo.
For a start, I am surrounded by fences,
and there is only one of me.
In the middle distance there are trees.

Who the hell are you
trying to kid? Definitely not me!
This is nothing like the plains,
and I am not a regular buffalo.
For a start, I am surrounded by fences,
and there is only one of me.
In the middle distance there are trees
and, on the horizon a couple of cranes.

Who the hell are you
trying to kid? Definitely not me!
This is nothing like the plains,
and I am not a regular buffalo.
For a start, I am surrounded by fences,
and there is only one of me.
In the middle distance there are trees
and, on the horizon, a couple of cranes
are in the process of building a block of flats.

Arctic Wolves, Lithuania, 2016

We are a pack of Arctic Wolves.
We are a pack of Arctic Wolves
in the process of losing almost everything.

We are a pack of Arctic Wolves.
We are a pack of Arctic Wolves
in the process of losing almost everything
that makes us what we are.

We are a pack of Arctic Wolves.
We are a pack of Arctic Wolves
in the process of losing almost everything
that makes us what we are;
caribou, raven, open spaces.

We are a pack of Arctic Wolves.
We are a pack of Arctic Wolves
in the process of losing almost everything
that makes us what we are;
caribou, raven, open spaces.
We are a pack of Arctic Wolves.

We are a pack of Arctic Wolves.
We are a pack of Arctic Wolves
in the process of losing almost everything
that makes us what we are;
caribou, raven, open spaces.
We are a pack of Arctic Wolves
unsure of where our prey is.

We are a pack of Arctic Wolves.
We are a pack of Arctic Wolves
in the process of losing almost everything
that makes us what we are;
caribou, raven, open spaces.
We are a pack of Arctic Wolves
unsure of where our prey is;
unsure of where our land is.

We are a pack of Arctic Wolves.
We are a pack of Arctic Wolves
in the process of losing almost everything
that makes us what we are;
caribou, raven, open spaces.
We are a pack of Arctic Wolves
unsure of where our prey is;
unsure of where our land is;
unsure if we are wolves at all.

Toucan, Croatia, 2016

I am about as high as I can
get, and yet, it is never enough,
I am always on my own.

I am about as high as I can
get, and yet, it is never enough,
I am always on my own,
perched on a wooden cross.

I am about as high as I can
get, and yet, it is never enough,
I am always on my own,
perched on a wooden cross,
underneath a skylight that is.

I am about as high as I can
get, and yet, it is never enough,
I am always on my own,
perched on a wooden cross,
underneath a skylight that is
my own glass ceiling.

I am about as high as I can
get, and yet, it is never enough,
I am always on my own,
perched on a wooden cross,
underneath a skylight that is
my own glass ceiling.
The world is somewhere.

I am about as high as I can
get, and yet, it is never enough,
I am always on my own
perched on a wooden cross,
underneath a skylight that is
my own glass ceiling.
The world is somewhere
out there; somewhere out there.

I am about as high as I can
get, and yet, it is never enough,
I am always on my own,
perched on a wooden cross,
underneath a skylight that is
my own glass ceiling.
The world is somewhere
out there, somewhere out there,
but always out of reach.

Feeder Mouse, Denmark, 2016

What a way for me to go,
and then, after I had gone, what
a way to find myself displayed.

What a way for me to go,
and then, after I had gone, what
a way to find myself displayed;
hanging upside down by my tail.

What a way for me to go,
and then, after I had gone, what
a way to find myself displayed;
hanging upside down by my tail,
attached by a bulldog clip to a twig.

What a way for me to go,
and then, after I had gone, what
a way to find myself displayed;
hanging upside down by my tail,
attached by a bulldog clip to a twig.
Being killed has somehow saved me.

What a way for me to go,
and then, after I had gone, what
a way to find myself displayed;
hanging upside down by my tail,
attached by a bulldog clip to a twig.
Being killed has somehow saved me
from the indignity of being a lifer.

What a way for me to go,
and then, after I had gone, what
a way to find myself displayed;
hanging upside down by my tail,
attached by a bulldog clip to a twig.
Being killed has somehow saved me
from the indignity of being a lifer,
but not from the ignominy of being.

What a way for me to go,
and then, after I had gone, what
a way to find myself displayed;
hanging upside down by my tail,
attached by a bulldog clip to a twig.
Being killed has somehow saved me
from the indignity of being a lifer,
but not from the ignominy of being
little more than someone else's meal.

Unknown Animal, Lithuania, 2016

I am what I am
and what I am is
unknown; no matter.

I am what I am
and what I am is
unknown, no matter
how hard you look.

I am what I am
and what I am is
unknown. No matter
how hard you look
you will never know.

I am what I am
and what I am is
unknown. No matter
how hard you look
you will never know
what I really am.

I am what I am
and what I am is
unknown. No matter
how hard you look
you will never know
what I really am;
being as I am.

I am what I am
and what I am is
unknown. No matter
how hard you look
you will never know
what I really am;
being, as I am,
the unknown.

I am what I am
and what I am is
unknown. No matter
how hard you look
you will never know
what I really am;
being, as I am,
the unknown
and the unknowable.

We polish an animal mirror to look for ourselves.
- Donna Haraway

Washed-Up Calf Corpse, Israel, 2018

Two weeks ago, hardly anyone had
even heard of me but now I have gone viral;
not much more than a bag of bones dumped at sea.

Two weeks ago, hardly anyone had
even heard of me but now I have gone viral;
not much more than a bag of bones dumped at sea
in the Med and washed up on a beach.

Two weeks ago, hardly anyone had
even heard of me but now I have gone viral;
not much more than a bag of bones dumped at sea
in the Med and washed up on a beach
in Tel Aviv. Not so long ago, I was just like you.

Two weeks ago, hardly anyone had
even heard of me but now I have gone viral;
not much more than a bag of bones dumped at sea
in the Med and washed up on a beach
in Tel Aviv. Not so long ago, I was just like you,
a living, sentient being, but now I am not.

Two weeks ago, hardly anyone had
even heard of me but now I have gone viral;
not much more than a bag of bones dumped at sea.
in the Med and then washed up on a beach
in Tel Aviv. Not so long ago, I was just like you,
a living, sentient being, but now I am not.
Now, I am unrecognizable as what I was.

Two weeks ago, hardly anyone had
even heard of me but now I have gone viral;
not much more than a bag of bones dumped at sea
in the Med and then washed up on a beach
in Tel Aviv. Not so long ago, I was just like you,
a living, sentient being, but now I am not.
Now, I am unrecognizable as what I was.
Now, I am nothing more than a visual image.

Two weeks ago, hardly anyone had
even heard of me but now I have gone viral;
not much more than a bag of bones dumped at sea
in the Med and then washed up on a beach
in Tel Aviv. Not so long ago, I was just like you,
a living, sentient being, but now I am not.
Now, I am unrecognizable as what I was.
Now, I am nothing more than a visual image
of what, because of you, I have become.

Acknowledgements

Some of the poems have appeared in the following publications and broadcasts:

Animal Culture (USA), The Blue Nib (Ireland), Confluence, The Ekphrastic Review (Canada), The Express Yourself Project, Foxglove Journal, Foxtrot Uniform, FTP Magazine, Greetings Anthology, The Honest Ulsterman, Impspired, Live Encounters (Indonesia), NatureVolve, North West Words (Ireland), The Open Mouse, The Poetry Village, Przekoj (Poland), Rochford Street Review (Australia), Southlight, The Seventh Quarry.

GREETINGS

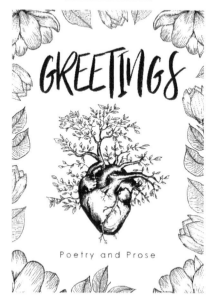

Featuring work by some of the UK's most exciting emerging artists, Greetings walks the thin line between love and loss in an examination of what it means to be human.

Desire and yearning take flight on windswept beaches and city streets, beneath crumbling monuments and monolithic office blocks. The dead are lamented, lovers are separated by distance, war and circumstance, and ancient family curses come to sinister ends.

In this inventive and powerful collection of poetry and prose, the reader is taken on a haunting and affective journey led by more than thirty new writers

ISBN: 978-1916113039

SNARES

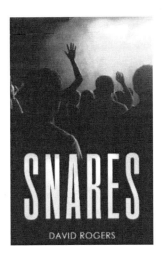

Having survived a gruelling and prolonged ordeal at the hands of his father, Sean becomes submissive to a dark presence; a manifestation of what he experienced as a child that influences him in ways he cannot control.

As reality and fiction begin to bleed into one another, Sean is forced to accept the only truth he has ever really known - that despite his greatest efforts, he will always be his father's son.

ISBN: 978-1-91611-300-8

STRANGE SEASONS

An elegant, heartfelt collection of poetry and prose from one of London's most exciting new writers – Stephanie Powell.

Strange Seasons offers a meticulously crafted and achingly beautiful perspective of life, love and loss that resonates long after the final page.

ISBN: 978-1-9161130-2-2

www.enthusiasticpress.co.uk

GORDON MEADE

GORDON MEADE is a Scottish poet based in the East
Neuk of Fife. He divides his time between his own writing
and developing creative writing courses for vulnerable
people in a variety of settings. *Zoospeak* is his tenth published
collection of poems.

JO-ANNE MCARTHUR

JO-ANNE MCARTHUR is a photographer, author, and the
founder of *We Animals Media*, which tells the stories of
invisible animals worldwide. She has spoken extensively on
the subjects of photography, animals, and social change.
Toronto, Canada is her home.

ISBN 978-1-9161130-4-6

9 781916 113046 >